THE CONTEMPORARY CONDITION

THE CONTEMPORARY CONDITION 08

On Writing a Literary History of the Contemporary, or What is, or was, "the Contemporary," and should we keep calling it that? Margaret-Anne Hutton

Published by Sternberg Press, 2018

© 2018 Margaret-Anne Hutton, Sternberg Press, Aarhus University and ARoS Aarhus Art Museum

Series edited by Geoff Cox & Jacob Lund

Published in partnership with ARoS Aarhus Art Museum and The Contemporary Condition research project at Aarhus University, made possible by a grant from the Danish Council for Independent Research, September 2015 – August 2018.

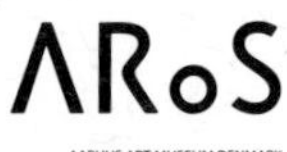

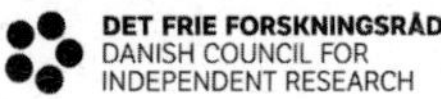

contemporaneity.au.dk

Many thanks to the Leverhulme Trust, whose funding of the International Network for Contemporary Studies has facilitated this publication.

Design: Dexter Sinister
Printing and binding: BUD Potsdam
Paper: Cyclus Offset

ISBN 978-3-95679-389-9

Sternberg Press
Caroline Schneider
Karl-Marx-Allee 78
D-10243 Berlin
www.sternberg-press.com

The Contemporary Condition book series offers a
sustained inquiry into the contemporary condition from a
range of perspectives by key commentators who investigate
contemporaneity as a defining condition of our historical
present. Contemporaneity refers to the temporal complexity
that follows from the coming together in the same cultural
space of heterogeneous clusters generated along different
historical trajectories, across different scales, and in different
localities. With the overall aim of questioning the formation
of subjectivity in time and the concept of temporality in the
world now, it is a basic assumption that art can operate
as an advanced laboratory for investigating processes of
meaning-making and for understanding wider developments
within culture and society. The series identifies three broad
lines of inquiry for investigation: the issue of temporality, the
role of contemporary media and computational technologies,
and how artistic practice makes epistemic claims.

SternbergPress

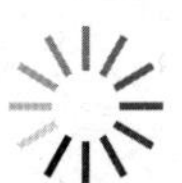

On Writing a Literary History of the Contemporary, or What is, or was, "the Contemporary," and should we keep calling it that?

Margaret-Anne Hutton

In the opening sentence of his *Brouhaha: Les mondes du contemporain* (2016),[1] one of the most sustained attempts to theorize "the contemporary" to date, Lionel Ruffel observes that for over a decade the question "What is the Contemporary?" criss-crossed various cultural and geographic spaces, from Rosario's Centro de Expresiones Contemporáneas in Argentina in 2004, to Stanford University in 2012, and the University of St Andrews in Scotland two years later, via what is perhaps still the best known iteration, the 2009 English translation of Giorgio Agamben's short essay *Che cos'è il contemporaneo?*.[2] Ruffel's use of tense — "Depuis dix ans, la question 'Qu'est-ce que le contemporain?' traverse les mondes et les langues" — implies continuity into the present, but do we in fact now know what the contemporary is?[3] I suggest that although the question has fallen away as a means of labelling an academic conference, exhibition, or text, the answer is far from clear, and that this is due in large part to terminological troubles: "The contemporary" as a noun suffers from semantic overload and ambiguous usage (it is used to mean both different things and too many things); this is compounded by the equally unstable use of other, related terms, such as "contemporaneity"; translation issues contribute further to lack of consistency; the relationship between "the contemporary" and the adjectival "contemporary" as used to qualify various disciplines requires some unpicking (the unacknowledged slippage from noun to adjective is widespread).

At least some of these terminological problems can be linked to the fact that "the contemporary" features in different discursive contexts: abstract, theoretical, and philosophical on

---

1. Lionel Ruffel, *Brouhaha: Les mondes du contemporain* (Lagrasse: Éditions Verdier, 2016), 7. An English translation is forthcoming at the time of writing: *Brouhaha: Worlds of the Contemporary*, trans. Raymond N. MacKenzie (Minneapolis: Minnesota Press, 2018). All translations of *Brouhaha* in what follows are mine.

2. Giorgio Agamben, *Che cos'è il contemporaneo?* (Milan: Nottetempo, 2008).

3. "For about a decade now the question 'What is the contemporary?' has been criss-crossing different spheres and languages."

the one hand; concrete, pragmatic, and discipline-based on the other (to simplify somewhat). With this in mind, theory and practice are deliberately entwined in what follows. I take as my starting point a concrete if apparently oxymoronic project: writing a literary history of the contemporary. A series of possible approaches to this hypothetical project is proposed in the opening section, with theoretical implications and objections bracketed out at this stage. A second section both traces the different definitions of "the contemporary" in the work of a number of theorists, and loops back to provide a metacritical commentary on the literary history project. With theory and practice thus informing one another, my aims are twofold: to provide a critical overview of how "(the) contemporary" is used as a term and what it variously designates, and to sketch out a self-reflexive take on what writing a literary history of the contemporary might involve, both because this is a project of value in its own right, and because it can also serve as an exemplar of how "the contemporary" might operate as a workable *critical* term.

A Hypothetical Literary History of
the Contemporary

Bearing in mind the deliberately unreflexive nature of this version, the chosen title for my hypothetical edited volume — or more likely volumes — will be *A Literary History of the Contemporary: From the Ancient Greeks to the 21st Century*. Of practical necessity this would be a comparative project, with contributors covering as broad a range of language, period, and geographical expertise as possible. The brief can be kept deceptively short and simple: primary texts should be selected and presented in such a way as to cast light on "the contemporary" as understood at various times and in various places. Justification of text selection and a clear vision of how framing material in the light of the contemporary contributes to original scholarship would be expected. At the risk of presentist projecting, I suggest that contributors might use various critical tools. They might draw on theoretical or philosophical works relating to, for instance, concepts of temporality, or "newness," or periodization. They might consider the contemporary in relation to other critical-aesthetic terms such as "avant-garde," or "modern(ist)." Contributors could make use of paratextual materials such as authors' prefaces and manifestos. They could turn to critical reviews, literary prizes, and journals and, especially, the remits that accompany these; to anthologies and their prefaces. And, of course, to literary texts themselves.

My first hypothetical chapter is based on Charles Perrault's "Le Siècle de Louis le Grand" (1687), selected because the context of the "Querelle des Anciens et des Modernes" suggests itself as a productive means of examining concepts potentially cognate to "the contemporary." How might this be approached? The text could of course be analysed in terms of the relationship between what it meant to be designated "Moderne" at the close of 17th-century France and prevailing notions of temporality and history. My hypothetical contributor might wish to consider "the contemporary" in relation to what the text itself reveals about notions of historicism: Is Louis XIV to be appraised on his own terms (in his own time) or in relation to Augustus? What can we make of the conditional tenses that project a version of how Homer *would have written* were he alive in Louis's time ("Ton génie [...] // Ne t'aurait pas permis tant de digressions")[4]? What of the suggestion that some writers are not recognized in their time ("Ovide était connu de sa seule Corinne")[5], or do not for long maintain their lustre ("À peine maintenant ces exploits singuliers // Seraient le coup d'essai des moindres écoliers")[6]? Which writers are contemporary, and of whom?

4. "Your Genius [...] // From such digressions would have stayed your hand" (my translation).

5. "To all but his Corinne remained unknown" (my translation).

6. "Today these singular exploits // Would be no more than callow schoolboys' first essays" (my translation).

Contexts can be seen differently. In a bold, apparently anachronistic statement, Joan DeJean has asserted that this was "the poem that launched the Culture Wars in 1687."[7] For Ruffel, the US Culture Wars and the related democratization of culture were some of the triggers of the birth of "the contemporary."[8] Perrault himself draws a distinction in his work between an elite ("des clients couronnés") and the less privileged masses ("l'ardente populace") as part of his attempt to validate the "Modernes" and their endeavours.[9] Might an extension of DeJean's comparison yield insights into both "Moderne" as it was then and "contemporary" as it is now? Pushing the comparison further, might we say, for instance, that the renowned "Ancien," Boileau, was the Harold Bloom of his time (in the latter's "canon wars" phase), and thereby potentially cast new light on both figures?

Perhaps "the contemporary" could be approached via periodization constructs. DeJean, after all, suggests that Perrault's poem redefined the term "siècle" : "*Siècle* means the age of Louis XIV, a period whose length was determined by that monarch's years, rather than by the fixed span of a hundred years."[10] What then is the relationship between this periodizing gesture and the designation "Moderne"? By extension, how is "the contemporary" as aesthetic linked to "the contemporary" as period? Might it usefully be considered as a *fin de siècle* phenomenon? It may be that Perrault's poetic articulation of the century could enter into productive dialogue with Agamben's reading of Mandelstam's "Le siècle" in *Che cos'è il contemporaneo?*, or with Alain Badiou's attempt to revisit periodization by offering various sequences (1890–1914, or 1917–1990, for instance) as possible

7. Joan DeJean, *Ancients against Moderns: Culture Wars and the Making of a fin de siècle* (Chicago: University of Chicago Press, 1997), 17.

8. Ruffel, *Brouhaha*, 13.

9. "Crowned heads" and "the ardent crowd" (my translation).

10. DeJean, *Ancients against Moderns*, 19.

twentieth-century period markers.[11] The notion of "the contemporary" as a period or periodizing concept is something to which we will return.

Finally, my hypothetical contributor might opt to focus on institutional factors contributing to constructions of "the contemporary." To what extent was the act of reading the "Siècle de Louis le Grand" to members of the *Académie française* a crucial part of the consecration of who was deemed to be "in," of "the now," and who had become (or just was) "passé"? There is a certain irony in the fact that Perrault's trumpeting of the timely should take place in an institution housing those known as *les immortels*, and that esteemed members — amongst whom Perrault himself numbered — should occupy their designated *fauteuil* until their death: a long shelf life indeed.

It is not my aim to develop these varied potential approaches here, but rather to set them up for further reflection and comment, either in the commentary sections below, or in other fora. For now, a chronological leap forward and a second hypothetical chapter, this time on the French "Nouveau Roman." The extent to which the "contemporary" can be equated to the "new," and how the latter is defined in any given place and at any given time, would inevitably be a part of my hypothetical literary history. (Armand D'Angour's *The Greeks and the New* could provide an early starting point.)[12] In the case of the "Nouveau Roman" the emergence and what I regard as the subsequent mythification of the designation is worth pursuing. The term "Nouveau Roman" is strongly associated with Alain Robbe-Grillet's *Pour un Nouveau Roman* (1963), comprising essays published between 1953 and 1963 and described by Pascale Casanova as a

11. Alain Badiou, *Le Siècle* (Paris: Seuil, 2005).

12. Armand d'Angour, *The Greeks and the New: Novelty in Ancient Greek Imagina-tion and Experience* (Cambridge: Cambridge University Press, 2011).

"manifesto" used to self-proclaim the author's status as "moderne."[13] A case can be made, however, that it was critics who had as much to say in creating the "Nouveau Roman" brand: "Le roman est à nouveau possible. *Un nouveau roman.* [...] Un roman sans mauvaise conscience, ni usurpation d'une impossible divinité" (italics in the original text).[14] This is Bernard Dort, writing in 1955. Other critics, taking up the label, were less well disposed, with Émile Henriot, for instance, regularly attacking this "new novel" in *Le Monde* over the course of the 1950s. Over four decades later Robbe-Grillet emphasized the critics' fashioning role:

> Le Nouveau Roman est rapidement apparu comme un ensemble négatif d'écrivains groupés par les reproches communs que l'ensemble de la critique leur faisait, et eux-mêmes finissaient par se définir comme luttant contre l'idéal que ces critiques défendaient.[15]

The intersection of different agential forces here is intriguing. To what extent were critics' views of what constitutes "proper" literature likely to have been a genuine influence on the novels being written as well as on their authors' self-designation? What different factors and agents might actually have combined to define the "newness"? According to Robbe-Grillet the "ideal" espoused by the critics of his time was embodied in one writer: Balzac. In a series of radio

---

13. Pascale Casanova, "Le méridien de Greenwich: Réflexions sur le temps de la littérature," in *Qu'est-ce que le contemporain?* ed. Lionel Ruffel (Nantes: Éditions Cécile Defaut, 2010): 126–27.

14. Bernard Dort, "Tentative de description," *Cahiers du Sud* no. 334 (1955): 364. "The novel is possible once again. *A new novel.* [...] A novel without a guilty conscience, which does not lay claim to an impossible divinity." (my translation).

15. *Alain Robbe-Grillet. Préface à une Vie d'Écrivain* (Seuil, 2005), 179. The volume, complete with CD, is an edited transcription of a series of radio interviews with Robbe-Grillet broadcast on France Culture between July 28 and August 29, 2003. "The New Novel soon began to seem like a negative group of writers brought together by the widespread criticism levelled against them by all the critics, and they too ended up defining themselves in terms of their struggle against the ideal defended by those critics" (my translation).

broadcasts in 2003 Robbe-Grillet was at pains to identify his own literary predecessors as Flaubert, Kafka, and Faulkner, seeing his work as a link in a process of inevitable evolution rather than a negative image of one dated writer. For all this, he could not help returning to the critics' measuring rod — Balzac — stating that a literary history could be written based on the analysis of the opening lines of novels, and citing Balzac and Camus as his case studies:[16] "Louis Lambert naquit en 1797 à Montoire, petite cité [sic] du Vendômois, où son père exploitait une tannerie de médiocre importance" (*Louis Lambert*); "Aujourd'hui maman est morte. Ou peut-être hier, je ne sais pas" (*L'Étranger*).[17] The comparison invites further thought about the role played by time, authority and succession in the construction of the contemporary. Does the deixis that marks Camus's incipit not also, after all, characterize the contemporary? In the case of Balzac, the opening sentence of *Louis Lambert* in full reads as follows:

> Louis Lambert naquit, en 1797, à Montoire, petite ville du Vendômois, où son père exploitait une tannerie de médi-ocre importance et comptait faire de lui son successeur; mais les dispositions qu'il manifesta prématurément pour l'étude modifièrent l'arrêt paternel.[18]

The fact that Robbe-Grillet's truncated quotation elides matters of succession and paternal authority is hard to ignore. Interestingly, although he bemoans the fact that critics sacralise certain writers (Balzac), he then uses these as points of comparison to condemn the new — "Je constate à ce

16. Robbe-Grillet, *Préface*, 22.

17. Ibid., 24. "Mother died today. Or maybe yesterday, I don't know." See note 18 for English translation of *Louis Lambert*.

18. "Louis Lambert was born at Montoire, a little town in the Vendomois, where his father owned a tannery of no great magnitude, and intended that his son should succeed him; but his precocious bent for study modified the paternal decision." Honoré de Balzac, *Louis Lambert*, trans. Clara Bell and James Waring (1832, repr., 2010) Project Gutenberg EBook.

moment-là que des formes littéraires ont été sacralisées comme si elles étaient éternelles"[19]—this, I would argue, is precisely what has happened to the Nouveau Roman. Note, for instance, the title of Tilby's *Beyond the Nouveau Roman: Essays on the Contemporary French Novel* (1990). Or Jean Duffy, arguing in her *Thresholds of Meaning: Passage, Ritual and Liminality in Contemporary French Narrative* that "both the writers of 'la nouvelle fiction' and the 'Ecole de Brive' define themselves in opposition to the nouveau roman."[20] These are just two of many similar cases. For a great number of critics and academics, the Nouveau Roman continues to act, even some six decades on, as a fixed point against which contemporary French literature is defined. How much longer, one wonders, can this go on?

Extending the focus on critics' constructions of the contemporary, my third contributory sketch is based on collected essays and anthologies which employ the term "contemporary" in their titles: for instance, remaining in the realm of French, Dominique Viart's *Anthologie de la littérature contemporaine: romans et récits depuis 1980* (2014). Viart's definitional criteria are clearly stated, if not justified to any extent: contemporary works are those that turn away from formalism and reengage with realism, whilst retaining a degree of self-reflexivity. Excluded from Viart's categorization are texts that demonstrate what he terms an "indifference towards literature," especially "popular" and genre fiction. Viart's "contemporary" designates both an aesthetic quality and a specific period: the texts that he chooses to anthologize started to emerge, he states, between 1975 and 1984.

This approach to the contemporary could take a hypothetical contributor in a number of directions. Should we, for example, be differentiating between the mechanisms whereby texts and authors are each labelled "contemporary"? Although

19. Robbe-Grillet, *Préface*, 112. "At this point I realised that certain literary forms have been regarded as sacred, as if they will last forever" (my translation).

20. Jean Duffy, *Thresholds of Meaning: Passage, Ritual and Liminality in Contemporary French Narrative* (Liverpool: Liverpool University Press, 2011), 3. My thanks to Kirsty Boardman for these references.

much of their work predates his 1975–84 periodization watershed, Viart includes *nouveau romanciers* (whom he dubs "dernières avant-gardes") in his anthology, on the grounds that their work underwent an aesthetic mutation during that period. This means that Robbe-Grillet can be simultaneously a contemporary and a not-contemporary author. Viart's division of his anthology into three parts invites further consideration of periodization. The opening section on the "dernières avant-gardes" is followed by a second on authors whose writing careers began in the 1975–84 period, whilst a third consists of a younger generation of writers deemed to be freed altogether from the burdensome legacy of past formalisms. Can we then talk of "the contemporary" in terms of biological generations, or has the acceleration of today's world in fact rendered such a concept redundant? Given the mechanisms behind technological generations, might we rather consider conceiving of periodization in terms of iterations?

And finally, politics. A rather hostile reviewer of Viart's anthology is keen to point out that the French Ministry of Education had a role to play in the volume's publication.[21] As "contemporary literature" finds its way into school and university curricula, it is inevitable that different vested interests in constructions of the contemporary come into play.

As a point of comparison, and going back in time nearly 120 years, a simple catalogue search yields Ferdinand Brunetière's *Nouveaux essais sur la littérature contemporaine* (1895).[22] Brunetière, who assumes his readers already know what contemporary literature is, makes no attempt to justify his choices and offers a surprisingly broad range of approaches: An essay that at first glance seems to be on the work of Bernardin de Saint Pierre (1737–1814) in fact

21. Etienne De Montety, "D'Ormesson, Orsenna, Nothomb. Une anthologie et beaucoup d'oublis!," *Le Figaro,* March 19, 2014, http://www.lefigaro.fr/livres/2014/03/19/03005-20140319ART-FIG00192-ecrivains-figurez-vous-dans-ce-manuel.php.

22. Ferdinand Brunetière, *Nouveaux essais sur la littérature contemporaine* (Paris: Calmann-Lévy, 1895).

assesses three biographies of the author published between 1891 and 1892; another engages with a truly contemporaneous work of literature, Paul Bourget's *La Terre promise* (1892); in "La Statue de Baudelaire" Brunetière considers whether the poet deserves to be thus honoured in the present day. Particularly intriguing is the opening sentence of the chapter on Leconte de Lisle, that begins as follows: "Lorsque le directeur de la *Contemporary Review* m'a demandé de parler à ses lecteurs du grand poète que nous venons de perdre."[23] The most recent meaning of "contemporary" listed in the Oxford English Dictionary (OED)—"4. a. Modern; of or characteristic of the present period; *esp.* up-to-date, ultra-modern; *spec.* designating art of a markedly *avant-garde* quality, or furniture, building, decoration, etc., having modern characteristics"—cites *The Contemporary Review* (1866) as the earliest example of this usage. Did Brunetière's "contemporain" carry the same meaning?

If my first two sample chapters centred on approaches to the contemporary via the terms *moderne* and *nouveau*, and my third turned to the use of the qualifier "contemporary" in the titles of an anthology and a set of critical essays, my final hypothetical chapter looks to a primary text which engages explicitly with the contemporary in the diegesis. "The theme of the conference was—for once!—not The Future. It was The Contemporary. This was even worse." These words from Tom McCarthy's novel *Satin Island* (2015) are those of the first person narrator, an anthropologist clearly familiar with the work of Paul Rabinow (McCarthy admits in his "Acknowledgements" that he has "shamelessly lifted" the latter's "brilliantly formulated thoughts on the notion of 'the contemporary'").[24] This opens the way to various approaches, most obviously a critical reading of the relationship between

23. Brunetière, *Nouveaux essais*, 157. "When the editor of *The Contemporary Review* invited me to speak to his readers about the great poet whom we have just lost" (my translation).

24. Tom McCarthy, *Satin Island* (London: Jonathan Cape, 2015), 92.

the novel and Rabinow's take on the contemporary as
articulated in his *Marking Time: On the Anthropology of
the Contemporary* and on-going project "Anthropological
Research on the Contemporary."[25] Does referencing Rabinow
necessarily make *Satin Island* contemporary? In what ways
do the literary and theoretical texts complement or undermine
each other in their constructions of the contemporary?[26]
Taking a related tack, *Satin Island* can be read in the light
of another theoretical text, Geoff Cox and Jacob Lund's
*The Contemporary Condition: Introductory Thoughts on
Contemporaneity & Contemporary Art*, that includes an
analysis of the contemporary and "real time":

> In contrast to the teleology of a progress bar, a throbber
> [e.g. buffer wheel] does not convey how much of the
> action has been completed and resonates with our under-
> standing of the real-time dynamics of the contemporary
> condition and the ambiguity of the temporal registers that
> are running seemingly at the same time.[27]

The cover of *Satin Island* consists of a buffer wheel symbol,
whilst McCarthy's narrator, whose thoughts often turn to
the temporal and the technological, is also fascinated by
the concept, stating at one point that "Everything becomes
buffering, and buffering becomes everything."[28] How do text
and theory interact in this instance, and would reading one
in light of the other contribute to our understanding of the
contemporary?

---

25. Paul Rabinow, *Marking Time: On the Anthropology of the Contemporary* (Princeton, NJ: Princeton University Press, 2008); http://anthropos-lab.net/.

26. Other recent literary works could be brought into play here: both Emmanuelle Pireyre's *Féerie générale* (Paris: Éditions de l'Olivier, 2012) and Deborah Levy's *Hot Milk* (London: Hamish Hamilton, Penguin Books, 2016), for instance, feature anthropologists.

27. Geoff Cox and Jacob Lund, *The Contemporary Condition: Introductory Thoughts on Contemporaneity & Contemporary Art* (Berlin: Sternberg Press, 2016), 22.

28. McCarthy, *Satin Island*, 69.

Moving beyond this, one might perhaps wish to explore the writing not of a literary *history* of the contemporary but rather of a literary *anthropology*. Amongst many other reflections on his discipline, McCarthy's narrator — who plies his trade in a corporate setting — discusses the problematic concepts of "field," "home" and "informant":

> If these people's [informants] background and culture are at base no different from your own [...] how should you interrogate them? What constitutes "interrogation" in the first place? In what way would it be staged?[29]

Similar questions centring on critical distance have been asked in relation to contemporary historiography (what distinguishes the historian from the journalist?) and the study of contemporary literature (are academic experts reduced to the role of reviewers?).[30] It may be that literary historians have things to learn from anthropological methodologies and epistemologies.

This brings to an end what can be considered heuristic outlines to chapters of a hypothetical literary history of the contemporary. I believe that all of these potential approaches would, if developed, contribute to individual subject disciplines as well as to new critical insights into "the contemporary." This pragmatic project, however, would benefit from an injection of self-reflexive critique.

Terminological Troubles and *Critical Commentary on the project A Literary History of the Contemporary*
Every word in the project title — *A Literary History of the*

---

29. Ibid., 22–23.

30. Theodore Martin, for instance, remarks that "Without the benefit of critical distance, the contemporary is likely to register only as blank space or blind spot, unavailable to the rigors of historical analysis," *Contemporary Drift: Genre,* *Historicism and the Problem of the Present* (New York: Columbia University Press, 2017), 4. See also Robert Eaglestone, "Contemporary Fiction in the Academy: Towards a Manifesto," *Textual Practice* 27.7: 1090–91.

Contemporary: From the Ancient Greeks to the 21st Century — including prepositions and articles, could of course be called into question, from the relationship between "the contemporary" and the literary to the linearity and successivity implied in the "from [...] to"; from the choice to start with the ancient Greeks to the use of the periodizing marker "21st century." Much has already been written both on new approaches to the writing of literary histories and on concepts of periodization, and I do not wish to rehearse such matters here. The following discussion will be limited to addressing issues with the project which arise specifically in light of an analysis of the terminology surrounding "the contemporary" in a sample of key theoretical/critical works.

At least four different uses of "the contemporary" in noun form appearing in recent (post-2010) theoretical works can be identified. First, it is employed as an abstract noun to designate a transhistorical concept — transhistorical in the sense of occurring in, and relative to, multiple historical contexts. Ruffel's definition reads as follows: "Le contemporain est un rapport au temps historique, c'est un mode d'être au temps. Il est ainsi transhistorique. Il y eut autant de contemporains que de moments historiques, qui furent tour à tour contemporains."[31] Compare this to Burges's and Elias's version in the introduction to their *Time: A Vocabulary of the Present*: "We assume that 'the contemporary' is a historically deictic term, indicative of a sense of presentness that has been felt by cultures of the historical past as well as those of the current moment."[32] The definitions differ in emphasis, and the second suffers from a symptomatic imprecision (especially in its appeal to affect, but also in the almost tautological "current moment"). Be that as it may, both versions suggest that every

---

31. Ruffel, *Brouhaha*, 17: "The contemporary is a relation to historical time, it is a mode of being in time. It is thus transhistorical. There existed as many contemporaries as there existed historical moments, which were in turn contemporaries."

32. Joel Burgess and Amy J. Elias, *Time: A Vocabulary of the Present* (New York: New York University Press, 2016), 3.

era has its own "contemporary" which has something to do with how the present is apprehended by human subjects. A third variant, expressed in a particularly pithy form, is provided by Cox and Lund, who state that "the contemporary" is "a modal or experiential category in the sense that it is a particular relationship to time and to history."[33]

Critical Commentary

(i) Taking "the contemporary" in this first sense — as a transhistorical concept designating an apprehension of time by human subjects — it would certainly be possible to write a history of the concept. Such a project might draw on a range of theoretical works as well as cultural products. Strictly speaking, however, if it were to be not just a history of the contemporary but a literary *history, then the explicatory and illustrative value of "literature" would presumably need to be set out by the editors, if not by individual contributors. There are, after all, other possible approaches. Consider, for instance, Peter Osborne's claim in a section of his* Anywhere or Not at All *entitled "The Global Transnational, or, the Contemporary Today" that "Art is a privileged cultural carrier of contemporaneity."[34] It seems likely that different cultural products (texts, buildings, music, internet sites etc.) are "privileged carriers" of different concepts of the contemporary at different times.*

(ii) A project based on "the contemporary" as transhistorical concept evidently presupposes that "the contemporary" or a cognate concept has existed, for the most part under different names, through the ages.

---

33. Cox and Lund, *The Contemporary Condition*, 9.

34. Peter Osborne, *Anywhere or Not at All: Philosophy of Contemporary Art* (London: Verso, 2013), 27.

Ruffel, who does point out that "the contemporary" has its own history, chooses in Brouhaha. Les mondes du contemporain *to limit the focus to the concept in its most recent iteration.*[35] *Theodore Martin states in his* Contemporary Drift: Genre, Historicism and the Problem of the Present *that the term "the contemporary" "invokes the history of its own institutional emergence and the even longer history of its historical meaning," and follows a similar path to Ruffel, turning primarily to recent texts.*[36] *Theorists of the contemporary, it might also be noted, often gesture towards the etymology of the words "contemporary," or "modern" (as I do myself, above, with respect to the OED's mention of* The Contemporary Review), *but this process is rarely, if ever, traced further back in time to the examination of other terms. The attempt not just to identify but also to* name *earlier "contemporaries" (i.e. cognate terms for cognate concepts) would play a crucial part in the putative literary history.*

(iii) Looking back to some of the case studies sketched out above, and taking "the contemporary" in its transhistorical sense, contributors might be expected to argue the case that, for instance, in Perrault's time, or Robbe-Grillet's (but how is "their time" to be delimited?) the terms "modern" and "nouveau" designated a modal relationship to "the present" which can productively be related to "(the) contemporary" as a cognate term. The varying constructions and valences of these modal relationships would be under scrutiny, as might the relationship between adjectives and nouns: Are the "modernes" displaying a mode of "modernité," however named? Can the same term be applied to the works

---

35. Ruffel, *Brouhaha*, 30.   36. Martin, *Contemporary Drift*, 3.

(œuvres modernes) without slippage of meaning? Is the "nouveau" as a qualifier of "roman" the same as when applied to "romancier"?

Returning to terminology, I suggest that using "the contemporary" to designate an abstract transhistorical concept seems somewhat counter-intuitive. Ruffel states that "Pour cette conception, il serait plus juste de parler de contemporanéité que de contemporain," though he does not follow through with this renaming in the rest of his book.[37] Whilst "contemporaneity" might indeed serve better in English too, this meaning is not part of current usage (the OED gives "fact of being at the same time as"). This is part of the problem: unlike critical-aesthetic neologisms — "dadaism" for instance — terms relating to "the contemporary" which are still in the process of entering a new critical lexicon cannot readily shake off their everyday meanings.

Equally troublesome in this case is the fact that "contemporaneity," like "the contemporary," is employed differently by different theorists. For Cox and Lund, for instance, contemporaneity — regarded as "a defining condition of our historical present" — designates "the temporal complexity that follows the coming together in the same cultural space of heterogeneous clusters generated across different historical trajectories, across different scales, and in different localities."[38] Peter Osborne, meanwhile, introduces a hyphen to signal the coming together of temporalities: "con-temporaneity, a coming together not simply 'in' time, but *of* times."[39] Terry Smith's "contemporaneity" seems broader still: "A concept defined as the multiplicity of ways of being in time, at the

37. Ruffel, *Brouhaha*, 17; "With respect to this notion it would be better to refer to contemporaneity rather than to the contemporary."

38. This statement appears on the first inside page of all of the volumes in "The Contemporary Condition" book series published by Sternberg Press and edited by Cox and Lund.

39. Osborne, *Anywhere or Not At All*, 17.

same time as others, right now, but also at earlier and future times, in ways that open us to other, non-modern temporalities (including indigenous knowing), and to other kinds of time."[40]

Such terminological lability — and these are just some examples — is tricky enough. Once translation is added to the mix, matters get yet more complex. Though potential problems are widespread, the discussion will be limited here to two examples from just one text, Agamben's *Che cos'è il contemporaneo?*, which was published simultaneously in Italian and French in 2008, appearing only a year later in the English version. Consider the following statements:

> Il "tempo" del nostro seminario è la contemporaneità.
> Le "temps" de notre séminaire est la contemporanéité.
> The "time" of our seminar is contemporariness.[41]

Quite apart from the translation of "tempo," echoed in the Italian "con*tempo*raneità," carrying over acoustically in the French "temps" and "con*tempo*ranéité," but lost in English, there is now a third critical term at play: "contemporariness." The decision not to go with "contemporaneity" in the English translation is not explained but is clearly a deliberate choice, given that it is more usual for Italian words with the suffix "eità" to transfer to "-ity" (e.g. homogeneity [omogeneità], simultaneity [simultaneità], spontaneity [spontaneità]). Interestingly, in a recording of a lecture given in English in 2007, that covers much of the same ground as the essay, Agamben at one point actually uses the word "contemporanity" [sic] then pauses, smiles and points at someone in the audience,

40. Terry Smith, "Defining Contemporaneity: Imagining Planetarity," *Nordic Journal of Aesthetics*, no. 49–50 (2015): 156–74.

41. Agamben, *Che cos'è il contemporaneo?*, 7–8; *Qu'est-ce que le contemporain?*, trans. Maxime Rovere, (Paris: Éditions Payot & Rivages, 2008), 7–8; "What is the Contemporary?" in *What is an Apparatus?*, trans. David Kishik and Stefan Podatella (Stanford, CA: Stanford University Press, 2009), 39.

before correcting himself and opting for "contemporariness."[42] Both "contemporaneity" (as we have seen) and "contemporariness" are of course part of English usage: the latter is given in the OED as "state or fact of being contemporary." The main point, however, is that the terminology in theoretical and critical works is extremely fluid. In fact, it is not just the translation of "contemporaneità" which might pose problems: however we choose to translate it, the term has a meaning (or meanings) specific to Agamben in this particular work. Contemporariness, in *Che cos'è il contemporaneo?*—or would it be more accurate to say in *What is the Contemporary?*—is a particular way of relating to one's own time (it is thus modal and transhistorical): "Contemporariness is, then, a singular relationship with one's own time, which adheres to it and, at the same time, keeps a distance from it."[43]

In Agamben's punning text, contemporariness is also, somewhat tautologically, the defining characteristic of "the contemporary": but what, or which contemporary? "The contemporary is he who firmly holds his gaze on his own time so as to perceive not its light, but rather its darkness."[44] Clearly we have moved away from "the contemporary" as an abstract noun. In this definition, "the contemporary" is an individual subject (male, it would seem), exemplified by Agamben's version of the poet-seer. Attempts to translate this contemporary introduce further terminological complexities:

> Di chi e di che cosa siamo contemporanei? E, innanzitutto, che cosa significa essere contemporanei?
> De qui et de quoi sommes-nous les contemporains?
> Et, avant tout, qu'est-ce que cela signifie, être contemporains?

---

42. Agamben, "On Contemporaneity," 2007, European Graduate School Video Lecture, 4 min., 40 sec., https://www.youtube.com/watch?v=GsS9VPS__gms.

43. Agamben, "What is the Contemporary?," 41.

44. Ibid., 44.

Of whom and what are we contemporaries? And first and foremost, what does it mean to be contemporary?[45]

In the French version the "contemporains" of "être contemporains" can function both as a plural *noun* and *adjective*, as it can in the source text but not, of course, in the English version. Again, beyond the terminological differences introduced by translation, Agamben's notion of "being contemporaries" is not straightforward, operating as it does to designate those who live in the same era (share the same time), but also those who have what we might call an aesthetic affinity, who are on the same wavelength, to switch metaphors. This sense emerges in the opening page of Agamben's essay, where he insists that "it is essential that we manage to be in some way contemporaries of these texts," the latter having potentially been written several centuries before.[46] Just how this is to be achieved remains unclear: "dovremo riuscire a *essere* in qualche modo contemporanei di questi testi" slips to "réussir à *nous faire*, d'une certaine manière, contemporains de ces textes" to the even more uncertain "we *manage* in some way to be contemporaries of these texts" (my emphases).

Critical Commentary

(i) Working on the basis that my hypothetical literary history of the contemporary will be written in English —a pragmatic assumption which should nonetheless not be taken lightly — it is clear that contributors should be required to display a highly reflective stance with respect to the use of translations of key terms, whilst editors would have to get to grips with a comparative overview of terminology. As suggested above in the

---

45. Agamben, *Che cos'è il contemporaneo?*, 7; *Qu'est-ce que le contemporain?*, 7; 'What is the Contemporary?', 39.

46. Agamben, "What is the Contemporary?," 39.

case of Brunetière's referencing of The Contemporary Review *in his own writing on "littérature contemporaine," we simply cannot take for granted that the near homophones "contemporary"/"contemporain" were semantic equivalents. By extension, we should not assume that the "Querelle des 'Anciens' et des 'Modernes'" translates — not just linguistically but culturally — as the "Quarrel of the 'Ancients' and the 'Moderns,'" or indeed that "'New' Novel" is an appropriate rendering of "'Nouveau' Roman."*

Note that Barbara Cassin's Dictionary of Untranslatables, *which focuses on philosophical terms and defines an untranslatable "loosely" as "a term that is left untranslated as it is transferred from language to language [...] or that is typically subject to mistranslation," does not include an entry on "contemporary" (or indeed "modern," though there is an entry on "present").[47] As Osborne points out, "contemporary" was not yet a critical term when Raymond Williams's* Keywords: A Vocabulary of Culture and Society *appeared in 1976.[48] Although the* New Keywords *(2005) also eschews an entry on "contemporary," the University of Pittsburgh's "Keywords Project," running between 2006 and 2016 does include an entry (not in the main list but a separate archive section), though there is no acknowledgement of the current lability of terms or discussion of what may be lost in translation.[49]*

47. Barbara Cassin, ed., *Dictionary of Untranslatables: A Philosophical Lexicon*, trans. and eds. Emily Apter, Jacques Lezra, and Michael Wood (Princeton, NJ: Princeton University Press, 2014), vii.

48. Osborne, *Anywhere or Not At All*, 16.

49. Tony Bennett, Lawrence Grossberg, and Meaghan Morris, eds., *New Keywords:* *A Revised Vocabulary of Culture and Society* (Malden, MA: Blackwell, 2005). Pittsburgh project, http://keywords.pitt.edu/index.html. An entry by Terry Smith entitled "Contemporary, Contemporaneity" can be found in the project archive ("contemporary" does not feature on the project's alphabetical list).

(ii) Agamben's notion that as readers we should be the contemporaries of texts "whose authors are many centuries removed from us" opens up different approaches to writing a literary history of the contemporary. The decoupling of the latter from the synchronous would, for instance, allow us to look again at one of my sample studies from a different perspective. Perrault ("Moderne") was the temporal contemporary of Boileau ("Ancien"), but not a contemporary in Agamben's sense of the term; the two were not in time with each other (a tempo), this in spite of the fact that both men saw themselves as reworking old forms for a new audience. The "Ancien," furthermore, was a satirist — what could be more aesthetically contemporary? The "Moderne" wrote in alexandrines. The "ancient"/"modern" binary might be prised further apart using the critical play of the contemporary.

(iii) If writers writing at the same time can fail to be contemporaries in Agamben's sense, then the opposite also holds true. There is scope, for instance, not (just) for a literary history of the contemporary, but a History of Literary Contemporaries. *Which authors, perhaps writing centuries before, might be identified as contemporaries in the Agambian sense by present-day writers such as Tom McCarthy, and what criteria would come into play? What role would be played by readers and critics in the designation of these cross-temporal contemporaries? Mapping such a constellation of literary contemporaries would reveal "live" links, active "conversations" taking place across time.[50] Working along similar lines, one might, as Vivian Liska has suggested, consider a* Literary History of the Untimely, *an exploration of when, and why,*

50. My thanks to my colleague Dr Robin McKenzie for developing this idea.

texts produced across the centuries 'achieve legibility' (to use Agamben's term at the close of Che cos'è il contemporaneo? *).*[51]

So far "the contemporary" has been seen to be used in critical works as an abstract noun designating a transhistorical modal concept. In Agamben's text it also defines a certain "untimely" person who experiences contemporariness (i.e. a visionary critical distance from his/her own time). In plural form, by extension, contemporaries are those who not only coexist temporally but are "a tempo" in aesthetic terms. The noun "the contemporary" is used in yet another way by scholars: to refer to a specific historical reality, i.e. ours (a problematic term in itself). Used in this way, and somewhat paradoxically, "the contemporary" refers to the latest historical iteration or instance of the transhistorical concept "the contemporary." Terry Smith's observation provides a useful starting-point:

> "The contemporary" is an adjectival phrase missing its noun. Ask always, "The contemporary [...] *what*?" In most cases you will find that the speaker is using an abbreviation for "the contemporary world," "our contemporary situation," "the contemporary condition," "the contemporary experience," or some such.[52]

In fact, as we have seen, "the contemporary" is not always best considered as "an adjectival phrase missing its noun"; in some cases it is best regarded as a nominalized adjective striving to attain the status of a critical-aesthetic term akin to,

51. Exchange with Professor Vivian Liska, June 2017.

52. Terry Smith, "Defining Contemporaneity: Imagining Planetarity," 167. In his *The Contemporary Composition* (Berlin: Sternberg Press, 2016), Smith refers to "the concept of 'the contemporary'" in many art worlds today as "a mindless vacuity, a mystification about the contemporary condition as somehow at once absolutely up to date and beyond historical time," 67.

for instance, "the sublime" or "the good." Having said that, Smith is right to suggest that "the contemporary" does operate as shorthand for "the contemporary world" (or other missing noun) when used by some critics in some contexts. In such cases we move from concept to instance, abstract to concrete, atemporal to temporally situated. When Ruffel subtitles his volume "Les mondes du contemporain," "le contemporain" ("the contemporary," if we translate in the most obvious manner) potentially designates both a transhistorical concept and the world in which we live now. The cover blurb to his book, however, stresses the latter, stating as it does that "un nom, *le contemporain*" (author's emphasis) is used to designate "un *nouveau* rapport au temps et à l'espace" (my emphasis).[53] The Aarhus University project "The Contemporary Condition" and book series of the same name edited by Cox and Lund also demonstrate this less abstract usage: "the contemporary" — sometimes qualified as "the contemporary contemporary" — designates "our historical present."[54]

For Lund and Cox this 'the contemporary' is characterized by 'contemporaneity,' as defined by them (in some contexts): that is, a coming together of different temporalities. Here we find referential, if not terminological, consensus amongst many theorists. For Osborne, the historical present is marked by the coming together of times in time — "con-temporaneity" — whilst Ruffel's (contemporary) contemporary is described in terms of "cotemporalité dans le présent de tous les temps historiques."[55] This temporally stratified contemporary in turn precipitates the need to reconsider concepts of successivity, innovation, and obsolescence. As Jussi Parrika puts it (slipping from "the contemporary" to "the contemporary condition" with no comment):

53. "One noun, *the contemporary*"; "a new relationship to space and time."

54. Cox and Lund, *The Contemporary Condition*, 9; see also their 2017 conference *The Contemporary Contemporary*, http://conferences.au.dk/contemporary2017/.

55. Ruffel, *Brouhaha*, 20; "cotemporality in the present of all historical times."

Let us start with a hypothesis that opens up the discussion about the contemporary in this text: The contemporary condition expands to a multitude of times that overlap and that cannot be resolved into one, simple designation such as "new" or "old."[56]

Critical Commentary

(i) One potential missing noun in the apparently truncated phrase "the contemporary" is, as Smith notes, "condition," with its nod to Lyotard's The Postmodern Condition. *A literary history of the contemporary would not be complete without an analysis of the relationship between the contemporary and the postmodern. Looking to terminology, it is worth pointing out that whilst there has been much debate surrounding the definitions and interrelations of the critical terms postmodern, postmodernity and postmodernism (and indeed modern, modernity, modernism), a single word "(the) contemporary" is currently obliged potentially to do the equivalent work of these triads and designate a socio-political condition, a historical period and set of aesthetic qualities, not to mention a transhistorical concept.[57]*

Beyond the question of terminology, contributors might usefully produce a comparative analysis of those

---

56. Jussi Parrika, *A Slow, Contemporary Violence: Damaged Environments of Technological Culture* (Berlin: Sternberg Press, 2016), 9.

57. Fredric Jameson has stated that if he could, he would now substitute the term "postmodernity" for "the postmodern," to emphasize the fact that "it was not a style but a historical period, one in which all kinds of things, from economics to politics, from the arts to technology, from daily life to international relations, changed for good": see Eric Bulson, "This is a headline," *TLS*, October 19, 2016, https://www.the-tls.co.uk/articles/public/this-is-a-headline/. See also Susan Friedman, "Definitional Excursions: The Meanings of Modern/Modernity/Modernism," *Modernism/Modernity* 8.3 (2001): 493–513.

critical terms that began to fill the vacuum left by the apparent academic demise of postmodernism. How do neo-modernism, meta-modernism, cosmodernism, post-postmodernism, planetarism — to name but a few — relate to the contemporary? One term in particular that seems to have gained critical traction is "the anthropocene." Foregrounding different temporal scales, technology, and the human species and operating across disciplines (itself a very timely phenomenon) is the anthropocene a category of the contemporary or does it bear some other relation to it (competitor, possible successor)? For Hyde and Wasserman, whose survey is largely limited to critical approaches to American literature, it represents just one of a number of ways in which the contemporary is conceived by literary critics.[58] *More work remains to be done on how different literary-based conceptions and categories of the contemporary interact and how, when, and why such different categorizations appear and disappear.*

(ii) Still working with the notion of the contemporary and/as the post-postmodern, and bearing in mind the notion of the contemporary contemporary (sic) as characterized by multiple coexisting temporalities, contributors might look to identify literary trends that seem to exemplify such a definition (I will have more to say on the relationship between literary texts and theorizing the contemporary below). In his Why Literary Periods Mattered *Ted Underwood explores what he terms "anxieties about historicism" as these are played out in parallel lives novels of the 1990s, identifying*

---

58. Emily Hyde and Sarah Wasserman, "The Contemporary," *Critical Compass* 14.9 (2017): 6–7. See also "Weather: Western Climes," in Martin, *Contemporary Drift*, 124–60, for a reading of the genre of the western in relation to concept of the contemporary and climate change.

these works as signs of the post postmodern.[59] Might it be that contemporary anxieties are manifested not in parallel lives novels (defined by Underwood as novels in which "[a]ctors, biographers, or critics set off on the trail of characters in an earlier historical period, who turn out to be in some sense their prototypes,"[60]) but alternative lives novels? Both Kate Atkinson's Life after Life (2013), with its stop-start overlapping temporal segments and Paul Auster's 4321 (2017) with its four versions of the life of Archibald Isaac Ferguson certainly challenge notions of periodization and a linear unfolding of time. Meanwhile, the Department of Diachronic Operations that gives Neal Stevenson and Nicole Galland's The Rise and Fall of D.O.D.O. (2017) its name, sets out to prevent the death of magic caused by photography, a demise that fixed historical time into one linear unfolding rather than a complex braid of different possible timelines.

(iii) If "the contemporary" is defined by its hetero-chronicity, its challenging of historicity, successivity, and linearity, then the structure of my hypothetical literary history project will require careful thought and justification — "from the Ancient Greeks to the 21st Century" will hardly do — and may require further renaming: Can it really still be called a "history" at all? (The same question can be asked of both the History of Literary Contemporaries and the Literary History of the Untimely outlined above.) Perhaps we should (pace Foucault, Benjamin, Didi-Huberman inter alios) refer to it rather as a literary archaeology of the contemporary, though it is worth noting that "real" archaeologists are questioning

---

59. Ted Underwood, *Why Literary Periods Mattered* (Stanford, CA: Stanford University Press, 2013), 136–56.

60. Ibid., 137.

*the role and value of the metaphor their discipline has
made available.*[61]

Two final interrelated issues remain. If "the contemporary"
is approached in terms of Smith's adjectival phrase missing
its noun, can that absent noun be "age" or "era"? Is "the
contemporary" a period? Secondly, what is—or should be
—the relationship between concepts of "the contemporary"
and the qualifier "contemporary" as applied to literature
(since my concern here is with a literary history)?

At the level of the conceptual, using one term—"the
contemporary"— to designate both a transhistorical concept
and a specific historical period is evidently problematic. A
definition of the contemporary emphasizing an "archaeological"
piling up of temporalities (a con-temporary or heterochronic
contemporary) that marks an end to linearity and successivity
also undercuts the notion of periodization. Equally troublesome
in theoretical terms is how the contemporary as period is to be
delimited, given its ever-unfolding and thus by definition non-
totalizable, nature. As the Raqs Media Collective put it, using a
pleasingly concrete metaphor, "The timetable for the contemporary ferry has not been published anywhere."[62] These
aporiae belong to the realm of theory. What happens when the
praxis of academic disciplines comes into play? A comparison of
Ruffel's take on the contemporary as period with that of historian Henry Rousso is instructive in this respect. Ruffel formu-
lates his objections by looking to the discipline of historiography:
based largely on European conflicts and events, period bound-
aries are noted to be Eurocentric and imperialist; start dates
vary (the history of the contemporary may be deemed to

61. See, for instance, the introduction to
Paul Graves-Brown, Rodney Harrison, and
Angela Piccini, eds., *The Oxford Handbook
of the Archaeology of the Contemporary
World* (Oxford: Oxford University Press,
2013) and Alfredo González-Ruibal, ed.,
*Reclaiming Archaeology: Beyond the Tropes
of Modernity* (London: Routledge, 2013).

62. Raqs Media Collective, *We Are
Here, But Is It Now? (The Submarine Hori-
zons of Contemporaneity)* (Berlin: Sternberg
Press, 2017), 13.

start in 1789, or 1914, or 1945, etc.); a lack of end date has seen the introduction of the new periodizing term "histoire du temps present," such that paradoxically "la période contemporaine appartient au passé."[63] Writing elsewhere, Rousso approaches exactly the same issues in a rather different spirit. Having noted the varied possible start dates and pointed out that alongside "histoire contemporaine" one can find not just "histoire du temps present" but also "histoire immédiate," the historian goes on to make the important distinction between a "practical definition" of contemporary contemporary history (his term) and "the more abstract notion of contemporaneity or contemporariness," adding that the practical and the theoretical can be mutually illuminating.[64]

Following on from this, I suggest that when working within the practical exigencies of an academic discipline, the need to consider terms relating to the contemporary as functional critical categories is imperative. In the following assertion by Peter Osborne I have replaced the word "art" with "literature" throughout:

> Perhaps the greatest barrier to a critical knowledge of contemporary literature, though, is the common-sense belief that the phrase "contemporary literature" has no *critically* meaningful referent; that it designates no more than the radically heterogeneous empirical totality of literary works produced within the duration of a particular present (our present); that it is, thus, not a proper part of a critical vocabulary at all.[65]

---

63. Ruffel, *Brouhaha*, 16-17; "history of the present time"; "the contemporary period belongs to the past." The same shift ever closer to the present moment can of course be found in literary criticism: note such titles as Amy Hungerford's *Making Literature Now* (Stanford, CA: Stanford University Press, 2016), or Warren Motte's *Fiction Now: The French Novel in the Twenty-First Century* (Champaign, IL: Dalkey Archive Press, 2008).

64. Henry Rousso, "Coping with Contemporariness," in Lia Brozgal and Sara Kippur, eds., *Being Contemporary: French Literature, Culture and Politics Today* (Liverpool: Liverpool University Press, 2016): 20.

65. Osborne, *Anywhere or Not At All*, 2.

There is no reason for literary scholars not to bracket out
the various ontological impasses relating to the contemporary
(Osborne's "contemporary" is indeed conceptualized as a
necessary fiction)[66] and to consider it in terms of a period, the
key consideration then being what critical *knowledge* doing so
would yield and what further questions would be precipitated.
In the case of, say, drawing up a module entitled "Contemporary French Fiction," or indeed producing a monograph or
academic journal of the same title, once the temporal parameters for "contemporary" have been set out and explained
— a process that would in itself be of interest — the need
further to justify text selection would remain: Some additional,
aesthetic, criteria would be required in order that the qualifier
"contemporary" have critical force. These criteria will emerge
from a mutually constructive interplay of literary texts and
concepts of the contemporary.

The nature of the interplay between concepts and texts,
and the degree to which this relationship is acknowledged,
vary. Emily Apter, for instance, uses the indeterminacy of
"the contemporary" as period marker as a way to challenge
historicizing approaches to literary history, asserting
mid-argument that "Literature, of course, provides endless
narrative experiments in the punctuation of experience,
often against the grain of historical time," and citing Ahmet
Hamdi Tanpinar, Roberto Bolaño, Orhan Pamuk, Ma Jian,
and Patrik Ouředník as authorial examples.[67] The specific
status and role of literary texts in the theoretical constructions
of the contemporary is hard to pin down here. In the case
of Ruffel, we see how some concepts of the contemporary
can lead to practical difficulties when it comes to identifying
"contemporary" literary texts. When Ruffel's "the contemporary" refers to our historical present characterized by a

66. Osborne, *Anywhere or Not At All*,
22–26.

67. Emily Apter, "Rethinking
Periodization for the 'Now-Time,'" in
Brozgal and Kippur, *Being Contemporary*:
34.

democratizing emphasis on the act of publishing — Ruffel states that "on passe d'un imaginaire de la littérature à un imaginaire de la publication, d'un imaginaire moderne à un imaginaire contemporain" — the focus falls upon user-generated texts such as blogs and fan fictions.[68] When "the contemporary" refers to the archaeological heaping up of times, the repertoire of literary texts in question necessarily expands to include a more traditional conception of literature (part of the "modern imaginary") as well as user-generated texts: "La Littérature n'est plus alors qu'une des actualisations possibles du littéraire et de la publication. Encore une fois: pas de substitutions, une addition."[69] Ruffel and Apter, perhaps because they are theorists above all, make little attempt *explicitly* to unpick the relationship between concepts of the contemporary and literary texts that are deemed to be contemporary. Martin, by contrast, makes his intentions and methodology clear from the outset of *Contemporary Drift*, which, he tells us, aims to produce "a survey of the narrative forms and critical practices that shape our varying conceptions of the contemporary."[70] Wasserman and Hyde, coming at things with similar intentions but from a different tack, do not set out to choose their own "contemporary" texts and concepts of "the contemporary" but rather to survey texts deemed to be "contemporary" by other scholars, and thereby to identify a common concept of "the contemporary."[71] Following from these examples, I suggest that if "(the) contemporary" is to function as a *critical* literary term, the nature of the link between theory and praxis, concept and concrete example, should always be explicitly articulated.

68. Ruffel, *Brouhaha*: 95; "we move from an imaginary based on literature to an imaginary based on publication."

69. Ruffel, *Brouhaha*, 106. "Henceforth Literature is merely one of the possible actualizations of the literary and of publication. Once again: no substitutions, just addition."

70. Martin, *Continental Drift*, 1.

71. Wasserman and Hyde, "The Contemporary."

Conclusions, For Now

In my introductory comments I suggested that the question "What is the Contemporary?" appears no longer to be employed in the context of labelling academic events, but that it nonetheless remains unanswered. The reasons for this have been identified as follows: both the conceptual and, more significantly, terminological lability surrounding "the contemporary" and its cognates; the exacerbation of this terminological ambiguity which is caused by translations of key terms (my examples, what is more, were limited to three European languages); the tension between conceptual aporiae and the need for "(the) contemporary" to have critical functionality within academic disciplines. In combining a hypothetical practical project — writing a literary history of the contemporary — with a focus on terminology and usage, I hope to have not just stated, but also demonstrated, the benefits of sustaining an explicit dialogue between the conceptual and the practical. However, whilst more reflective practice and attention to linguistic and cultural translation may go some way towards clarifying what both "contemporary" as applied to academic disciplines and "the contemporary" as a concept, condition, person or period may signify, I remain concerned by the terminological burden placed upon a single word and its cognates.

My terminological anxiety is, I believe, part of a wider phenomenon. Insistent repetition of the question "What is the Contemporary?" in the years following 2004 may have ceased, but it seems that the repetitive compulsion, a symptom of continued epistemic uncertainty, has merely been displaced and reconfigured. Between 2015 and 2017 a significant number of projects relating to "the contemporary," featuring across different disciplines and practices, have produced or otherwise referenced the need for dictionaries, glossaries and lexicons. The following is a sample. Berlin's Haus der Kulturen der Welt project, "100 Years of Now" (2015–2018), includes a "Dictionary of Now" which sets out to redefine key words (from "Animal" to "Violence").[72] Joel Burges's and Amy J. Elias's *Time* (2016) is subtitled "*A Vocabulary of the Present.*" The series "Theorizing the Contemporary" run by *Cultural Anthropology*, the journal of the Society for Cultural Anthropology, includes a "Lexicon for an Anthropocene as Yet Unseen."[73] Heidi Quante and Alicia Escort's online participatory artwork "The Bureau of Linguistic Reality" focuses on "creating new language as an innovative way to better understand our rapidly changing world due to manmade climate change and other Anthropocenic events."[74] Camille de Toledo, Aliocha Imhoff, and Kantuta Quirós's *Les Potentiels du temps* (2015), a manifesto for a better future based on an analysis of our "contemporary condition," ends with a glossary complete with a cross-referencing system reminiscent of the eighteenth-century *Encyclopédie*.[75] Finally, Raqs Media Collective's *We Are Here, But Is It Now? (The Submarine Horizons of Contemporaneity)* states: "We do not really know the A, B, and C of the present moment. We need a new alphabet for now," going on to suggest a series of neologisms to circumscribe aspects of the contemporary condition: "presentomorrow," "dromosapien," and "memery," for instance.[76]

This "new alphabet of now" should, I believe, include terms not just for phenomena that are part of "the contemporary condition," but for "(the) contemporary" itself. Some degree of terminological consensus is surely required in order that the emergent field of contemporary studies function effectively and expand. It is unlikely that critics and practitioners will buy into neologisms. In the spirit of starting a conversation,

72. http://www.hkw.de/en/programm/projekte/2015/woerterbuch_der_gegenwart/woerterbuch_der_gegenwart_start.php

73. https://culanth.org/field-sights/803-lexicon-for-an-anthropocene-yet-unseen.

74. https://bureauoflinguisticalreality.com/about/

75. Camille de Toledo, Aliocha Imhoff, and Kantuta Quirós, *Les Potentiels du temps* (Paris: Manuella éditions, 2016).

76. Raqs Media Collective, *We Are Here, But Is It Now?*, 16, 41–47.

I nonetheless propose the following combination of old, new,
and repurposed English-language, terms: "contemporaneity,"
a transhistorical modal concept expressing a human subject's
apprehension of the historical present; "contimely," occuring
at the same time as; "contimeliness," the phenomenon of
occurring at the same time as; "the contemporary + noun," to
describe a world, condition, experience, etc., where "contemporary" has deictic force; "contemporariness," a term used by
Agamben which might be replaced by "untimeliness"; "heter-
ochonic"/"heterochronicity," the coming together of several
temporalities; a possibly defining characteristic of the world
post Web 2.0. Of course the emphasis here remains predomi-
nantly temporal. Perhaps it is time to change this, too.

BIBLIOGRAPHY

Agamben, Giorgio. *Che cos'è il contemporaneo?* Milan: Nottetempo, 2008.
——. "What is the Contemporary?" In *What is an Apparatus?*, translated by David Kishik and Stefan Podatella. Stanford, CA: Stanford University Press, 2009.
——. *Qu'est-ce que le contemporain?* Translated by Maxime Rovere. Paris: Éditions Payot & Rivages, 2008.

d'Angour, Armand. *The Greeks and the New: Novelty in Ancient Greek Imagination and Experience.* Cambridge: Cambridge University Press, 2011.

Apter, Emily. "Rethinking Periodization for the 'Now-Time.'" In *Being Contemporary*, edited by Brozgal & Kippur. Liverpool: Liverpool University Press, 2016, 29–42.

Atkinson, Kate. *Life After Life.* London: Doubleday, 2013.

Auster, Paul. *4.3.2.1.* London: Faber & Faber, 2017.

Badiou, Alain. *Le Siècle.* Paris: Seuil, 2005.

Bennett, Tony, Lawrence Grossberg, and Meaghan Morris, eds. *New Keywords: A Revised Vocabulary of Culture and Society.* Oxford: Wiley-Blackwell, 2005.

Brozgal, Lia and Sara Kippur. *Being Contemporary: French Literature, Culture, and Politics Today.* Liverpool: Liverpool University Press, 2016.

Brunetière, Ferdinand. *Nouveaux essais sur la littérature contemporaine.* Paris: Calmann-Lévy, 1895.

Bulson, Eric. "This is a Headline." *TLS*, October 19, 2016. https://www.thetls.co.uk/articles/public/this-is-a-headline/.

Burgess, Joel and Amy J. Elias, eds. *Time: A Vocabulary of the Present.* New York: New York University Press, 2016.

Casanova, Pascale. "Le méridien de Greenwich: Réflexions sur le temps de la littérature." In *Qu'est-ce' que le contemporain?*, edited by Lionel Ruffel. Nantes: Éditions Cécile Defaut, 2010, 113–45.

Cassin, Barbara, ed. *Dictionary of Untranslatables: A Philosophical Lexicon.* Translations edited by Emily Apter, Jacques Lezra, and Michael Wood. Princeton, NJ: Princeton University Press, 2014.

Cox, Geoff and Jacob Lund. *The Contemporary Condition: Introductory Thoughts on Contemporaneity & Contemporary Art.* Berlin: Sternberg Press, 2016.

DeJean, Joan. *Ancients against Moderns: Culture Wars and the Making of a Fin de Siècle.* Chicago: University of Chicago Press, 1997.

De Montety, Etienne. "D'Ormesson, Orsenna, Nothomb. Une anthologie et beaucoup d'oublis!" *Le Figaro,* March 19, 2014. http://www.lefigaro.fr/livres/2014/03/19/03005-20140319ARTFIG00192-ecrivains-figurez-vous-dans-ce-manuel.php.

de Toledo, Camille, Aliocha Imhoff, and Kantuta Quirós. *Les Potentiels du temps.* Paris: Manuella éditions, 2016.

Dort, Bernard. "Tentative de description." *Cahiers du Sud* no.334 (1955): 355–64.

Duffy, Jean. *Thresholds of Meaning: Passage, Ritual and Liminality in Contemporary French Narrative.* Liverpool: Liverpool University Press, 2011.

Eaglestone, Robert. "Contemporary Fiction in the Academy: Towards a Manifesto." *Textual Practice* 27.7 (2013): 1089–1101.

Friedman, Susan. "Definitional Excursions: The Meanings of Modern/Modernity/Modernism." *Modernism/Modernity* 8.3 (2001): 493–513.

González-Ruibal, Alfredo, ed. *Reclaiming Archaeology: Beyond the Tropes of Modernity.* London: Routledge, 2013.

Graves-Brown, Paul, Rodney Harrison, and Angela Piccini, eds. *The Oxford Handbook of the Archaeology of the Contemporary World.* Oxford: Oxford University Press, 2013.

Hungerford, Amy. *Making Literature Now.* Stanford, CA : Stanford University Press, 2016.

Hyde, Emily and Sarah Wasserman. "The Contemporary." *Critical Compass* 14.9 (2017): 1-19.

Levy, Deborah. *Hot Milk.* London: Hamish Hamilton, 2016.

Martin, Theodore. *Contemporary Drift: Genre, Historicism and the Problem of the Present*. New York: Columbia University Press, 2017.

McCarthy, Tom. *Satin Island*. London: Jonathan Cape, 2015.

Motte, Warren. *Fiction Now: The French Novel in the Twenty-First Century*. Champaign, IL: Dalkey Archive Press, 2008.

Osborne, Peter. *Anywhere or Not At All: Philosophy of Contemporary Art*. London: Verso, 2013.

Parikka, Jussi. *A Slow, Contemporary Violence: Damaged Environments of Technological Culture*. Berlin: Sternberg Press, 2016.

Pireyre, Emmanuelle. *Féerie générale*. Paris: Éditions de l'Olivier, 2012.

Rabinow, Paul. *Marking Time: On the Anthropology of the Contemporary*. Princeton, NJ: Princeton University Press, 2008.

Raqs Media Collective. *We Are Here, But Is It Now? (The Submarine Horizons of Contemporaneity)*. Berlin: Sternberg Press, 2017.

Robbe-Grillet, Alain. *Alain Robbe-Grillet. Préface à une vie d'écrivain*. Paris: Seuil, 2005.

Rousso, Henry. "Coping with Contemporariness." In *Being Contemporary. French Literature, Culture and Politics Today*, edited by Lia Brozgal and Sara Kippur. Liverpool: Liverpool University Press, 2016, 15–28.

Ruffel, Lionel. *Brouhaha. Les mondes du contemporain*. Lagrasse: Éditions Verdier, 2016.
———. *Qu-est-ce que le contemporain?* Nantes: Éditions Cécile Defaut, 2010.

Smith, Terry. "Defining Contemporaneity: Imagining Planetarity." *Nordic Journal of Aesthetics*, no. 49-50 (2015): 156–74.
———. *The Contemporary Composition*. Berlin: Sternberg Press, 2016.

Stevenson, Neal and Nicole Galland. *The Rise and Fall of D.O.D.O.* London: The Borough Press, 2017.

Underwood, Ted. *Why Literary Periods Mattered: Historical Contrast and the Prestige of English Studies*. Stanford, CA: Stanford University Press, 2013.

Margaret-Anne Hutton is Professor of French and Comparative
Literature and Director of the Institute for Contemporary and
Comparative Literature (http://iccl.wp.st-andrews.ac.uk/)
at the University of St Andrews. She has published monographs
on French authors Michel Tournier and Christiane Rochefort,
on the testimonial accounts of French women deported during
WWII, and on representations of WWII in French crime fiction
as well as a number of edited volumes and shorter pieces on
contemporary literature. She is currently principal investigator
of a Leverhulme International Network entitled "What is the
Contemporary?" (https://arts.st-andrews.ac.uk/lincs/),
and is working on a range of contemporary-related publications.

PEN = 0, 40, 2, 22, WEIGHT = 100, SLANT = 0, SUPERNESS = 0.72

The typeface used to set this series is called Meta-the-difference-between-the-two-Font (MTDBT2F), designed by Dexter Sinister in 2010 after MetaFont, a digital typography system originally programmed by computer scientist Donald Kunth in 1979.

Unlike more common digital outline fonts formats such as TrueType or Postscript, a MetaFont is constructed of strokes drawn with set-width pens. Instead of describing each of the individual shapes that make up a family of related characters, a MetaFont file describes only the basic pen path or *skeleton* letter. Perhaps better imagined as the ghost that comes in advance of a particular letterform, a MetaFont character is defined only by a set of equations. It is then possible to tweak various parameters such as weight, slant, and superness (more or less bold, Italic, and a form of chutzpah) in order to generate endless variations on the same bare bones.

Meta-the-difference-between-the-two-Font is essentially the same as MetaFont, abiding the obvious fact that it swallows its predecessor. Although the result may look the same, it clearly can't be, because in addition to the software, the new version embeds its own backstory. In this sense, MTDBT2F is not only a tool to generate countless PostScript fonts, but *at least equally* a tool to think about and around MetaFont. Mathematician Douglas Hofstadter once noted that one of the best things MetaFont might do is inspire readers to chase after the intelligence of an alphabet, and "yield new insights into the elusive "spirits" that flit about so tantalizingly behind those lovely shapes we call "letters.'"

For instance, each volume in The Contemporary Condition is set in a new MTDBT2F, generated at the time of publication, which is to say *now.*

Dexter Sinister, 29/06/18, 11:55 AM